VOODOO

VOODOO

BY KYLE KRISTOS

J.B. LIPPINCOTT COMPANY   Philadelphia and New York

The pictures on pp. 10 and 11 are reprinted by courtesy of The Museum of Modern Art, Film Stills Archive, New York, N. Y. from *I Walked with a Zombie*. Copyright 1947, RKO Radio Pictures, Inc.

The picture on pg. 61 is reprinted by permission of Schocken Books Inc. from *Voodoo in Haiti* by Alfred Metraux. Copyright © 1959 by Alfred Metraux.

U.S. Library of Congress Cataloging in Publication Data

Kristos, Kyle.
  Voodoo

  Bibliography: p.
  Includes index.
  SUMMARY: Traces the origins, cults, and practices
which surround voodooism including voodoo practices in
the United States and modern Haiti.
  1. Voodoosim—Juvenile literature. [1. Voodooism] I. Title
BL2490.K72   299'.6   76-18989
ISBN-0-397-31706-9   ISBN-0-397-31707 (pbk.)

TO THE BEAUTIFUL
AND FRIENDLY PEOPLE
OF HAITI

ACKNOWLEDGMENTS

The author wishes to make grateful acknowledgment to President Duvalier of Haiti, M. Gaby Demarais, M. and Mme. Max Beauvoir, M. Theo Duval, M. Petitcoeur, and M. Lamartiniere Honorat.

CONTENTS

Veve for Ayizan

1
WHAT IS VOODOO?

Voodoo. At once the word brings to mind the dark mysteries of black magic, the frenzied rites of witch doctors, and the fearful, mindless creatures who are called zombies. These common associations with Voodoo have been fostered for decades by Hollywood films that stress the lurid, bizarre qualities of what is thought to be Voodoo.

To many, the word itself has a strange sound and even a rather strange look on the printed page; it is a word that can't be taken too seriously—a word that looks just as odd and questionable as the activities it stands for. Perhaps we should begin by finding out where the word comes from.

There is a good deal of confusion about the origin of the word *voodoo.* Most authorities believe that

Scenes from *I Walked with a Zombie* (RKO). In many films of this type, Hollywood emphasized the lurid aspects of Voodoo.

it comes from Dahomey, one of the major geographical areas in West Africa from which slaves were imported to the West Indies. Among the Fon—one of the tribes of the area—the word *vodun* is best translated as "god." It is related to the word *vo*, which means "apart." And so the word *vodun* suggests

something which is "godlike," something which is
"set apart and holy." Many people who write about
Voodoo prefer the word *vodun* and some use another spelling such as *vodoun* or even *voudoux*.

Still other writers claim that *voodoo* is of French
origin. A member of the Catholic clergy, Father Val-
desius, founded a sect in the twelfth century which
was called Vaudois. Eventually *vaudois* came to be
a term used to describe sorcerers and practitioners of
black magic, and some people believe the term was
brought to Haiti by early French colonists.

11

Further complicating the matter is the word *hoodoo*. This is a variation of *voodoo* which is sometimes used among American blacks but is not found in any other part of the world. Since *voodoo* is the word most commonly used, it is the term we shall use in this book.

More important than the origin of the word is its meaning, but this, too, leads us into a certain amount of confusion. The people of Haiti, the main center of Voodoo practice, consider themselves good Roman Catholics. But they also believe in what can be called the folk religion of Voodoo—a system of worship that has never been codified. Primarily, Voodoo is deeply concerned with the occult, especially with spiritism and possession.

The occult is that which is hidden from sight and involves the use of divination, incantation, spiritism, possession, and magical formulas. Magic itself is said to bring results from the use of supernatural forces that can be turned to good or evil.

Spiritism—which is sometimes called spiritualism—is communication with the ghosts of the dead. It is also concerned with any power they are able to manifest in the world of the living.

Possession is the use of a living body by another spirit, which may be that of a dead person or an entity, perhaps a god, from the realm of the supernatural.

All of these practices are a part of Voodoo. Many

Voodoo priests and priestesses also claim that they can see into the future. They prescribe medicines and other measures to cure illness and to prevent its occurrence. They prepare charms and talismans to help someone who is seeking the love of another person, while other charms and magical objects are provided for destructive purposes. Voodoo priests and priestesses are deeply concerned with the dying, with the realm of the dead, and with their effect on the living.

Voodoo involves all of this and more. It—like the occult—wears many faces. Voodoo is a mysterious and fascinating force in the lives of millions of people. In different forms and under different names it is practiced today in parts of Africa, some Caribbean islands, Brazil, and Louisiana. In this book, however, we will be talking about Voodoo as it is practiced in Haiti. Let's begin with its arrival in the Western Hemisphere many centuries ago.

The first black men and women to set foot in Haiti arrived in the year 1510. They were captives of Spanish settlers and were used as a labor force on the settlers' plantations. The Spanish, who named the island Hispaniola, slaughtered most of the native Indians, called Arawaks, in less than twenty years. When the Spanish ceded the island to the French in 1697, the latter changed the name to Saint Dominique. The French greatly expanded the plantation system, establishing huge sugar and coffee plantations which required the work of thousands of slaves. As the need for laborers increased, more and more blacks were brought from Africa. During Haiti's history as a plantation colony over nine hundred thousand black slaves were imported.

The slaves were treated like animals and were so brutalized that fresh shipments were continually needed to replace those who died as they worked in the fields. The slaves were viewed only as a means to profit, and no efforts were made to train or educate them.

One of the men who visited Haiti during this period wrote, "For the Negroes work starts before dawn. At eight o'clock they get their breakfast. They go back to work until midday when they are fed again. At two o'clock they start again and carry on until nightfall, sometimes right up to ten or eleven P.M." Often the two hours of free time they were permitted in the middle of the day were given over to the cultivation of their own food.

The men and women who were forced into slavery came from many different tribes in West Africa. Although their customs, culture, and language were similar, there were also great differences in their backgrounds. Once in Haiti, they were forced to live together, to work together, and often to die together.

The slaves came from many classes and included many different types of people. Some of them were criminals forced into slavery as punishment and some were prisoners who had been taken in tribal wars. Wealthy and even royal persons also found themselves on slave ships bound for Haiti. It sometimes happened that problems arose among the heirs of a tribal chief or king. To settle the dispute, finally and for all time, the son who was successful in attaining the throne disposed of any possible future threats to his power by selling his brothers, and their wives and children, into slavery. Priests and magicians sometimes met the same fate. It was through this mixed group of people that African religion and culture were brought to the new world.

However, African religion now took a new form. In Africa, the Ibos, Senegalese, Congos, Dahomeans, and other groups had worshiped in many ways and given different names to their gods. Each of their rituals had its own individual characteristics. In Haiti the various practices of the different tribes formed into one and became the heart of what is called Voodoo.

The Spanish and French colonists feared Voodoo and tried to suppress it from the earliest times. They considered it a "terrible weapon" and thought it to be a force which could rally the slaves to revolt. But the fear of Voodoo was based on more than its supposed ability to unite and inflame the slaves. The colonists knew that magic and control of supernatural forces was a part of its teaching, and they feared it on a personal level as well. Belief in the power of witches, demons, and werewolves was strong in Europe at that time and the colonists wanted no part of these frightful figures in any form. For these reasons Voodoo was suppressed, and slaves who were found to possess any Voodoo symbols or objects were punished with lashings, imprisonment, or hanging.

Nevertheless, the teaching of Voodoo was passed from one generation to another by priests who had become slaves. Although driven underground during periods of persecution, Voodoo surfaced during times when the determination of the authorities slackened. It was in this manner that Voodoo, through centuries of oppression, remained alive and eventually flourished on the island of Haiti.

The Catholic clergy have made serious attempts to stamp out Voodoo throughout Haiti's history. At certain periods the beating of the drums was strictly forbidden and any temple that came to the attention of Church authorities was destroyed immediately. One writer recalls that during a visit to Haiti in 1941 he saw "vast pyramids of drums, painted bowls, necklaces, talismans—all waiting for the day fixed for the joyous blaze which was to symbolize the victory of the Church over Satan."

But to the average Haitian there is nothing contradictory in being a good Catholic and a believer in Voodoo. As one old woman put it, "To serve the loa you have to *be* a Catholic." Catholicism and Voodoo are so closely interwoven in Haiti that to most Haitians they appear to be one and the same.

This mixture of Christianity and African religion developed gradually during the early colonial period and has continued to the present time. Orthodox Christianity is observed on Sundays and its rituals are practiced at times of death, baptism, and marriage. Several Catholic ideas and names have become a part of the Voodoo rituals. Many of the rituals begin with Catholic prayers.

As a summary of the way Catholic and Voodoo doctrines merge together in Haiti it might be said that the average person believes in God as the ruler of the universe and the creator and sustainer of all life. To carry through with His divine plan He created Jesus Christ and the Holy Catholic Church with its hierarchy and saints. Human beings have souls which come from God and return to Him for judgment after death.

Voodoo enters the picture because it is believed that the Catholic system does not give men and women direct contact with God and His supernatural forces. It is the loa who serve this function. According to Voodoo, the loa are lesser gods who are deeply concerned with the existence of human beings on earth and their fate after death. Voodoo teaches that every person has one loa who is his chief protector and whom he must honor above all others.

It is the loa, through Voodoo rituals, that make

the supernatural forces accessible to man. The loa represent these forces in a tangible, personal form that the average man can comprehend. They are an essential channel, which must be maintained at all costs, to the mysterious, unseen world. Therefore, it can be said that the average Haitian is a devout believer in the Catholic religion for whom the practice of Voodoo has a deep and pervasive influence on all levels of life from the moment of birth until death.

Although Voodoo was introduced to many islands in the West Indies, it took a strong and permanent hold only in Haiti. In Jamaica as well as some other islands of the Indies a form of Voodoo is practiced which is called Obeah. In Brazil still another variation of Voodoo's teachings is called Macumba.

However, it is Voodoo as practiced in Haiti that has become best known throughout the world. A great many books and articles have been written about it. Ethnologists have made several studies of Voodoo and Haitian life. Out of all this material have come many contradictory views of Voodoo and its influence.

One of two facts which cannot be challenged is that Voodoo has long been, and continues to be, an important force in the life of the average Haitian. Secondly, interest in Voodoo has grown steadily throughout the world. It holds a particularly strong fascination for people who are curious about psychic phenomena and mysticism.

As Voodoo developed, three distinct rites or groups emerged. The Rada rite is followed by the largest number of people in Haiti. Less is known about the Petro rite, which has its own loa who are thought to be stronger than the Rada loa and sometimes dangerous. Some writers connect the Petro rite to the Red Sect, which is described later in this book. The third Voodoo rite is called Congo.

Veve for
Ogoun Badagris

2

TEMPLES, PRIESTS, AND PRIESTESSES

You might pass a place where Voodoo rites are held and see nothing more than a clearing surrounded by trees, shrubs, and flowers. More often, however, Voodoo ceremonies are held in a temple called an *oum'phor* or a *peristyle*. The latter is a roofed enclosure open on the sides. Rites may be celebrated in either one or both of these structures, although dancing usually takes place in a peristyle.

Some writers believe that the design of the peristyle is similar to the plan used by Moses to build the Tabernacle, as described in Exodus in the Old Testament. To many it may seem odd to find the name of Moses connected with Voodoo. Yet, according to Voodoo tradition, Moses himself was initiated into Voodoo's mysteries. This legend maintains that Moses married Sephora, the daughter of his black teacher in Voodoo, whose name was Jethro. From this union came two mulatto sons, Gershom, whose name means "I dwell in a foreign country," and Elizer, whose name means "Help of God."

According to this legend, when Moses built the first Hebrew temple in Jerusalem, he planted his staff in the place where the centerpost of a Voodoo temple is still erected today. It is considered the holiest place within the Voodoo compound.

The temple, or sanctuary as it is sometimes called, can have one or several rooms. If it is a larger temple, there will be a room where those who wish to be initiated will be examined and taught the mysteries of Voodoo. This room looks like a tomb because Voodoo, like many other religions and cults, maintains that an initiate must first undergo a symbolic death before he or she can be reborn to true knowledge.

In the temple many activities take place. It is here that the priest or priestess calls the loa to come and take possession of the worshipers. In the temple prayers and incantations are sung. It is in the temple that the famous Voodoo dances are held, and it is also in the temple that the animal sacrifices take place.

There is much confusion about the men and

Primitive Haitian painting showing dancers at a Voodoo ceremony. All ceremonies are held on earthen floors, which are beter for making contact with the loa than those of wood, stone, or cement. The designs in the foreground are called veves.

women who lead Voodoo rituals. Some people call them priests but others refer to them as sorcerers. Still other people believe that those who are in charge of Voodoo ceremonies are witches, magicians, or witch doctors. Perhaps all of these names can be used to describe Voodoo practitioners. Let's see exactly what each of them means.

One definition of *priest* is "one of the clergy as distinguished from the laity." Using this definition, Voodoo leaders are priests, for they most definitely stand apart from their followers.

Although the word *sorcerer* is not used very often to describe the leaders of Voodoo, this word, too, may be a justified description. The word *sorcerer* is derived from the Latin word *sors* or "fate." A sorcerer, then, is one who attempts to control the fate of men and women through magic rituals and words. That is certainly a function of the leader of a Voodoo cult.

Already we have used the word *magic* and seen that it describes part of the work of a sorcerer or magician. But what exactly does *magic* mean? The word itself is of ancient origin. It comes from the Magi or wisemen of Persia, who could cast spells, control supernatural forces, and change the lives of people by using secret powers. Since this describes the work of a Voodoo cultist, *magician,* too, may be used as a name which applies to his or her position.

A witch is one who practices magic and is

thought to possess supernatural powers. The term *witch doctor* is simply a variation of *witch* and is usually applied to tribal practitioners of magic. In either case a witch is one who practices magic and possesses supernatural powers. It would seem that *witch* also can be used to describe the leader of a Voodoo cult.

Perhaps there is even another name which can be given to the practitioners of Voodoo. Necromancy is the calling up of the dead and a person who practices this is called a *necromancer*. Since those involved with Voodoo must have dealings with the dead, this word can also be used as an apt description.

And so it can be seen that each of the foregoing terms can be used as a description of the men and women who are the highest practitioners of Voodoo. These terms help us understand their very special position in the community and their enormous power.

However, the terms *priest, sorcerer, magician, witch doctor,* and *necromancer* suggest other figures in literature and history who are quite different from Voodoo cult leaders. It is perhaps best to call these men and women by the names they are given in Haiti.

A male Voodoo priest is called a *hungan.* As the highest personage in Voodoo, he is thought to be a person who understands many mysteries about life, the world of unseen forces, and the realm of death.

He is an interpreter of what the gods and the lesser deities wish to have happen here on earth. The hungan is a kind of link between men and gods; his knowledge and training have given him an understanding of the forces of life and death which few men possess. It is this long training that enables him to speak to the gods.

Usually the hungan uses his power for good. He intercedes for men and women who wish help from the gods. He knows the special rituals which must be performed to achieve the results desired.

In some temples the highest position of power is held by a female priest who is called a *mambo*. According to some writers on Voodoo, the mambo is not as powerful as the hungan, but others see the hungan and mambo as equal. The mambo, like the hungan, has great prestige in the community and often makes considerable profit from Voodoo activities.

The hungan is often called "papa" and the mambo may be called "mamman." Both hungan and mambo act as priests, confessors, doctors, and magicians to those who gather around them. Sometimes they are asked for advice on family matters. Other common concerns are love, death, birth, property rights, and prosperity.

The realm of death is especially important. Believers in Voodoo think that some of the dead can be very powerful. They fear the dead and turn to the hungan or mambo to contact the dead and to protect them from the dead.

Beneath the hungan or the mambo are several other people who assist them in their work. Directly below is the *la place,* an apprentice who knows the secrets of the hungan and may one day be a hungan himself. Beneath the la place is the *houngenicon,* who may be either a man or woman. The houngenicon is one of the special servants of the hungan and knows much about Voodoo rituals and ceremonies.

A hungan and mambo prepare offerings to the loa at the beginning of a Voodoo ritual.

Under these assistants are still others called *hounsi, bossale,* and *hounsi kanzo* who are lower in importance. They are learning about Voodoo as they assist in whatever way they can.

Both hungans and mambos are called upon to cure disease and illness. Some claim they can cure any disease by just passing the head of a freshly killed dog over the swollen or diseased area of the body. Others use more complex treatments.

There are a great many rituals which may appear to be a strange blend of mumbo jumbo and superstition to those who know nothing of Voodoo. And yet, hungans and mambos may be making use of psychological techniques that help the patient cure himself. Many studies have shown that sugar pills can achieve remarkable cures when given to some sick people who believe they are receiving medication. Perhaps the Voodoo practitioner is making use of the same principle, or perhaps, as believers in Voodoo claim, it is actually the loa who perform the healing.

Here are some of the specific treatments used: For rheumatism and arthritis a patient is sometimes locked in an empty room with a live turkey. The patient must stay all night in the room, and it is thought that by morning the disease will have passed to the animal.

Insanity is treated by a blend of white rooster feathers, special herbs and roots, finely crushed bones, and home-brewed rum. This mixture, which is believed to cure all mental disorders, must be stored in a mule's hoof until needed.

For a general illness that cannot be exactly diagnosed the following treatment is used: First a shallow hole that looks something like a small grave is dug in the ground. Then three pint jars of rainwater and three pint jars of red wine are placed in the hole. The ground around the hole is decorated by a design called a *veve* that is made in a checkerboard pattern. Only cornmeal is used to make the veve. A clean mat made of reeds, rushes, and straw is placed over the hole and the veve. The mat is sprinkled with sesame seeds. Then a stake of wood is driven into the ground at one end of the mat and a cross of any material at the other.

When all this has been finished, the sick person must lie down on the mat and relax as completely as possible. A rooster is then placed between his or her legs. The legs and the rooster are covered with a white sheet and sprinkled with salt. After that is done, twenty-one lighted white candles are placed on the ground in groups of seven. Prayers are sent to the loa Marinette. When one hour has passed, the cock must be taken away in a sealed black box and carefully buried in a secluded place.

Voodooists believe that the rooster has absorbed the illness of the sick person and that when the magic rite is over he or she will be completely restored to health.

An asson, or ritual rattle. There are no seeds or stones inside the calabash; a sound is produced by rattling the snake vertebrae against the outside of the calabash. The major loa are represented by the intersections of the vertebrae strands. In the background is a well sacred to the loa Damballah. Such wells are usually found near Voodoo temples.

Hungans and mambos own certain objects which are used in the rituals they conduct. The most important is the *asson* or ritual rattle. It is made from the gourd of a calabash and encased in the vertebrae of a snake which have been worked into a decorative design. With it the hungan or mambo makes invisible drawings in the air. It is also used to indicate the practitioner's wishes to his or her assistants.

Held in the hand that wields the asson is a small bell that is also used to call the loa. In some parts of Haiti whistles are used instead. Two important objects in every temple or sanctuary are flags which are made of silk or velvet and heavily spangled with glittering sequins. The flags are brought out at the beginning of a ritual and are carried among the dancers.

On the altars are also bottles and dishes holding charms, various powders, and foods. Some of the powdered foods, especially cornmeal, are used to create the veves which are used in all Voodoo rituals.

Veves, which are traced upon the ground, are made with great care. The veve is a decorative design incorporating symbols which stand for supernatural forces. Once it is finished it is valueless. It is only the process of making it which calls the mystical powers into existence. Usually veves are destroyed by the rituals that follow their making, and if the ritual itself does not finish them off, the dancing which usually takes place is sure to do so.

Veve for
Agassu-Hayman

3
POSSESSION AND THE LOA

Possession—which is sometimes called "trance" —is an important part of religious ceremonies in many parts of the world and in many cultures. For many Voodooists it is an extraordinary experience which they believe gives them contact with the mysterious worlds of gods, spirits, and other mystic forces. Most of those who are possessed believe that the gods, or superhuman beings, are speaking through them.

Is possession hallucination or a kind of mass hypnosis? Some writers feel certain that it is. But some of the most recent scientific discoveries suggest that there are many forces in the world which men are just beginning to understand. However, whether possession is hallucination, mass hypnosis, or the visitation of a supernatural being, it *is* a central, undeniable part of the Voodoo experience. Let us listen to an explanation of trance that might be given by an authority on Voodoo in Haiti.

According to the teaching of Voodoo, every person carries two vital forces, sometimes called souls, within him- or herself. The *petit bon ange* (little good angel) can be compared to what Christians call the spirit. It is the divine animating power which gives the body life. The *gros bon ange* (big good angel) can be thought of as the shadow, or double, of a person. When possession takes place the gros bon ange leaves the body.

The beginnings of trance everywhere throughout the world are indicated by trembling, convulsions, and erratic body movements; the Voodooist explains this as the reaction of the gross physical body to the exit of the good big angel. Then the person who is possessed feels a sense of emptiness, as though he were fainting. The calves of his legs tremble and sometimes the irises of his eyes move partially under his eyelids.

When possession takes place the person no longer can control himself because in a sense he is not there. His body temporarily belongs to the loa who now inhabits it. From this point on, it is the loa who speaks through him, who moves him, whose temperament is shown by his facial expressions. The possessed has become an instrument of the loa.

The relationship between the loa and the possessed is often compared to that of a horse and rider. For this reason the loa is often spoken of as "mounting" his horse. The analogy can be carried further, for many horses become alarmed at finding themselves under the control of a new master and react unpredictably.

As possession takes hold of the person, he appears to have lost control of his motor system. He pitches forward and looks as though he is about to fall. His body stiffens as he turns around and may seem to move uncontrollably to the side and the rear. He pants heavily and sweats profusely and often a look of suffering and great tension can be seen in his face.

People who are accustomed to being possessed usually pass quickly through the symptoms just described. After a brief time of staggering and shaking or lurching they move into the period of full trance.

It is believed that the length of the opening period of the trance is also determined by the nature of the loa who seeks to possess. Gentle loa are said to enter the possessed gently. Powerful, strong, or cruel loa take possession with great force. Those who know Voodoo well have an idea of which loa is taking possession by observing these opening phases carefully.

As possession occurs, the onlookers watch

closely. They reach out and try to help those who are about to fall. Hungans and mambos try to help those who may cause themselves some physical injury. Objects of apparel that might be damaged or cause damage—such as hairpins, rings, and shoes—may be removed.

When possession is complete the person acts in an entirely new manner. He is usually dressed as the loa who has taken possession. Many Voodoo temples have a room containing much clothing and other adornments that can be used to dress possessed persons. Since sometimes male gods possess women and female gods possess men, the correct clothes must be put on by those in trance. When appropriate, men are put into dresses and made up as women and women find themselves wearing trousers and top hats.

Because the possessed no longer exists as a person, he is no longer responsible for his actions. For this reason people in trance can make outrageous or obscene comments and can do things which they would never do if they were in control of themselves. Occasionally people in trance try to deliberately hurt themselves. Possession appears to give believers in Voodoo a chance to live briefly in a way that is totally unlike their ordinary lives. Psychologists have observed that this provides a good channel for the Voodooist to express tensions which might find a less socially acceptable outlet if Voodoo did not exist.

Possession can also occur during ordinary daily life but this is rare. Some observers believe that people who find themselves in disagreeable or unbearable situations will suddenly go into trance as a means of escape. It is difficult to know if this is genuine trance or an imitation which offers a technique for survival.

The word *loa* comes from the French word *lois*, meaning "laws." In this sense the loa are the power of certain laws which can be used by those who have knowledge of the laws and the ways to use them.

The loa are sometimes referred to as gods, but generally their position is thought to be somewhere between humans and the higher gods. Like Catholic saints, they take an active concern in the welfare of those who pray to them. The loa are willing to help when they are called on, provided they have been honored in the various ways that are important to them. When not worshiped in the proper ways, they can, unlike Christian saints, punish the offender severely.

If asked about the loa, the average Voodooist might reply, "The loa love us, protect us, and guard us. They tell us what is happening to our relations who live far away, they suggest remedies to use which bring us relief when we are sick . . . if we are hungry the loa appear to us in a dream and say: 'Take courage—you will earn money,' and the promised money comes! . . . The loa warn us if anyone wishes to do us harm and they will rush to our aid if we are in need."

No one can possibly know the name of every loa in Haiti, for there are many hundreds of them. Some are famous and important, such as Damballah and Legba, and they, of course, are known throughout the island. Others are obscure and found only in certain small sections of the country. Some loa are known only to one family and its friends. It is thought that one's ancestors can become loa and provide help when called upon, and it is for this reason that the cult of the dead is extremely important in Haiti.

True believers in Voodoo are certain that the loa are always watching and listening, even though they remain unseen. They can also be thought of as powerful forces moving throughout the universe that can be channeled when the appropriate means are used. They are abstract and personal at the same time. And on the personal level they can be vengeful and cruel if they are not treated with respect. In Haiti it is believed that the slightest little thing can make the loa angry. Their rituals must be done with great care and they must always be given the food they like.

No one must ever resist the will of a loa. To do so is to ask for trouble. Punishment may not be swift but it will certainly come in time. People who have had a run of bad luck are certain that the loa are angry with them for something they have done. Illness, madness, constant poverty, and many other ills are thought to be the will of the loa in Haiti.

Following are brief descriptions of some of the most important loa:

DAMBALLAH—THE SERPENT GOD

In his fascinating book *Life in a Haitian Valley*, Melville J. Herskovits writes of Damballah, sometimes referred to as Da, "It would seem that Da is an abstraction, used to designate anything sinuous, which moves silently, undulates, and cannot be controlled. It is the principle of movement, of energy, of life itself, and, by extension, of fortune. Often spoken of as a serpent, Da is nevertheless the principle of mobility."

The serpent has been a very important symbol in many cultures and religions throughout the world. In Voodoo the serpent is a symbol of fertility—the source of life and the life principle that sustains all life. Voodoo gives the name Da to the serpent, which is said to be the oldest of the ancestors.

Da—whose full name is Damballah Houe-Do— is of such great age and so sacred that he does not speak in words but expresses himself through the hissing sound characteristic of the serpent. Whenever this sound is imitated during a voodoo ritual, it is Da speaking.

Veve for Damballah

Damballah is the most powerful of the loa, but he is never thought of as a father to the gods in the same way that Zeus or Jupiter was a father in Greek or Roman mythology. And yet it is believed that when any of the other gods meet him they bow and sing, "It is our father who passes." This is a gesture to his great importance and senority, but generally he is regarded as an enveloping force of life, instead of as a god with human attributes.

As such he is the great source of good things and power. The most respected and venerable of all the Haitian loa, he is a symbol of virility. It follows naturally that he is the loa of rain and springtime—the fertilization of the mother earth and the beginning of life. All trees are resting places for Damballah, because snakes climb trees. He is also the lord of rivers and marshes.

It is strange that the picture of Damballah people in Haiti often buy is actually that of St. Patrick. He does not look anything like St. Patrick, but there happen to be prints showing St. Patrick with snakes, and these are the pictures that are bought. Because the serpent is such an important part of Damballah's legend, it is understandable that people think the snake is worshiped in Haiti. In fact, it is greeted with respect and revered only as a symbol of the great Damballah and his power.

Damballah's color is white and food which is offered to him must be predominately white. He likes eggs, cornmeal, melons, rice, bananas, and grapes. There is often a dish on Damballah's altar which holds desserts, sweet liqueurs, and olive oil. Wednesday is his day, and his sacrifice is usually a pair of white fowl—a hen and a cock. Some people believe this is because Damballah is the god of married happiness and he will be certain to keep a married couple happy if they pay their respects to him in this way.

When people are possessed by Damballah they stick their tongues out and dart them from one side to the other. They crawl on the ground and climb trees or the supports of buildings. Sometimes, hanging on to the roof with their legs, they let their bodies fall down like snakes. Since Damballah does not speak but whistles, they make strange staccato sounds something like "tettetete . . ."

A Song to Damballah

Serpent, serpent-o,
Damballah-wedo papa,
You are a serpent.
Serpent, serpent-o,
I will call the serpent.
The serpent does not speak;
Damballah papa you are a serpent.
If you see a snake
You see Aida-wedo.

VOODOO

If you see a snake
You see Damballah.
Aida-wedo is a snake.

LEGBA

Legba is one of the great loa. He is thought to be the master of the mystic barrier which divides men from spirits and the world of reality from the unseen worlds. He is the chief god of all rituals. He is the god who "opens the gate." When a ceremony begins, the hungan chants, *"Papa Legba, ouvri barrie pou nous passer."* (Open the way for us to pass.) Believers are certain that if Legba grants their plea they will be able to make contact with the mysterious forces of the universe.

Since Legba must be present to give his approval or blessing to every ritual, some people ask how he can be in so many places at the same time. To this believers answer, "Christ is also called to help people all over the world. His mystic powers enable Him to do this and, in the same way, Legba can appear to many at the same time."

And so, to the Voodooist, Legba can be summoned to open the way to supernatural experience. Many prayers begin, "By thy power, Master of the

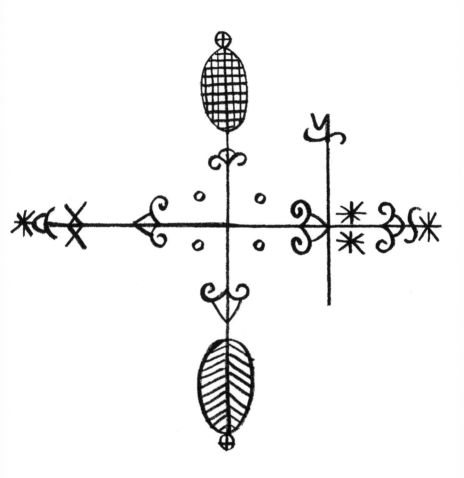

Veve for Legba

Crossroads." While this is descriptive of Legba in a philosophic or mystical sense, Legba is also master of the real crossroads. He is the god of gates and fences and also protects the home. When going on a journey, Voodoo believers pray to Legba to protect them from harm and to permit them to return home safely.

Legba is thought to be a kind, wise old man who is deeply loved. He is also represented as a weak old man dressed in rags. With his pipe in his mouth and a knapsack over his shoulder, he moves with difficulty on the road and often uses a crutch. For this reason he is sometimes called Legba of the Broken Foot.

Tuesday is his sacred day, and his plant is the plum tree. He likes to eat a certain type of rooster that is marked in many colors like a guinea fowl. In Haiti almost every man tries to sacrifice a male goat to Legba at least once in his lifetime.

Some people believe that Legba is even stronger than Damballah, and no Voodooist will drink *clairin* —a home-brewed rum drink—without first pouring out a drop on the ground for Legba.

A Song to Legba

Atibon-Legba, remove the barrier for me, agoe!
Papa Legba, remove the barrier
So I may pass through.

VOODOO

When I come back I will salute the loa.
Voodoo Legba, remove the barrier for me
So that I may come back;
When I come back, I will thank the loa, Abobo.

ERZULIE

It is Erzulie Freda—sometimes called the Virgin of the Voodoo gods—who expresses the female energy of Legba. She is a pleasure-loving, demanding, and sensuous loa who symbolizes all feminine grace and beauty. Erzulie-Freda loves blue and red dresses, jewels, and makeup. In every Voodoo temple there is a room or corner of a room which is dedicated to her; it is there that her cosmetics and other articles are kept. These usually consist of a bowl, soap, a toothbrush, a comb, and lipstick.

Although Erzulie can take human form, she is also known as a serpent that is usually coiled upon itself and lives mainly on water and bananas. Her supernatural powers are represented by the two serpents which she holds, one in each hand. As a serpent goddess she has tremendous power and is feared as much as she is loved and courted.

Maitresse Erzulie—as she is sometimes called—has several different roles. She is the goddess of the

Veve for
Erzulie

word, so that a person who wishes to speak well, to have a large vocabulary and beautiful speech, prays to Erzulie. She is also the loa of love, help, goodwill, health, beauty, and fortune. Since these objectives are important to all people, Erzulie is often given objects and attentions that will make her notice the believer.

At the same time, Erzulie is the loa of jealousy, vengeance, and discord. Especially in matters of love, Erzulie can cause great pain and many problems.

As soon as Erzulie possesses someone, even if the possessed is a man, that person is led to the place where her things are kept and is dressed in her clothes. Once dressed, the possessed person, whether male or female, will walk with a mincing gait and swing his or her hips provocatively. Often the person who is possessed gets presents from the men who are in the temple.

A Song for Erzulie

Ah, the lovely woman
Who is Erzulie!
Oh, I will give you a present
Before you go away, Abobo.

VOODOO

AGWE

Agwe is a loa of the sea, a water divinity whose color is blue and who is represented by a small boat. He is concerned with the elements; the flora and fauna of the sea; fishermen, sailors, and all others whose work or interests take them to the sea. Often he is shown as a mulatto with fair skin and green eyes, and he wears the uniform of a naval officer, with white gloves and a helmet. When Agwe is called during a Voodoo ritual, a conch shell is often used. His wife is La Sirene, the sea aspect of the goddess of love, Erzulie.

A Song to Agwe

Maitre Agwe, where are you?
Don't you see I'm on the reef?
Maitre Agwe, where are you?
Don't you see I'm on the sea?
I've a rudder in my hand;
I can't go back.
I'm already going forward;
I can't turn back.
Agwe-taroyo, where are you?
Don't you see I'm on the reef?

Veve for Agwe

GHEDE

One of the most important and greatly feared of all the loa, Ghede is a symbol of death. He is part of the large Ghede family of loa, all of whom are concerned with the end of life and the mysterious worlds beyond death. When Ghede takes possession of someone at a Voodoo ritual, the other loa leave and celebrants who are in a trance come out of their state of possession. They must do this because the loa, like human beings, do not mingle with the dead.

While Ghede is the loa of death, he is also the loa of resurrection. There is a strong erotic quality about Ghede and other members of the family, all of whom love obscene jokes relating to sex. Why should this be so? Perhaps we can look for an explanation to the Western tradition of the wake, a time of eating and often high spirits in what has been an atmosphere of sorrow and mourning. Death is fearful to most human beings, and the eating and singing during a wake are an affirmation that life still exists and will be perpetuated. Perhaps in a similar way Ghede's love of obscenity and his general interest in sexual matters are also an affirmation of life in the midst of death.

The hungan Max Beauvoir suggests that Ghede's disrespect and sexual vulgarities are aimed at puncturing the general conception of death as a state to

Veve for Ghede

be feared. Ghede reminds us that our understanding of life and death is limited and that both states of being are part of a whole beyond the comprehension of most human beings.

Saturday is Ghede's day, and black is his color. He is fond of salt herring, hot peppers, roasted corn, roasted bananas, and other roasted foods. Black goats and chickens are sacrificed to him.

A Song to Ghede-Brave
(A member of the Ghede family)

I say brave-o,
Call him brave! He's a bold fellow.
His banana end is bold,
His bit of chicken is bold,
His bowl of clairin is bold,
His bit of sweet potato is bold.
I call Brave-Ghede;
Come and save the children.
Brave-o, he's called brave!
He's a bold fellow.

BARON SAMEDI, BARON CIMETIERE, BARON LA CROIX

These loa can be thought of as aspects of Ghede or lesser loa in the Ghede family. They are all feared by Voodoo believers, for they rule the cemetery and other aspects of death. But like Ghede himself they also love to use obscene language, usually in a joking manner.

The clothing they wear—such as top hats, formal black suits, and starched cuffs—makes them look somewhat ridiculous, but, at the same time, they are terrifying to believers in Voodoo. The barons usually wear glasses.

Copies of two drawings found on the walls of Voodoo temples. On the left is Baron Samedi, loa of death and one of the Ghede family of loa. An unidentified death loa is on the right.

Veve for drums and for Ogan

4
A VOODOO RITUAL

It is night in Haiti and the trade winds are rustling the palm tree branches while the soft air is fragrant with the sweetness of thousands of flower blossoms. The night is very dark, for outside the capital of Port-au-Prince and a few other towns, there is little electricity in the countryside. Even within Port-au-Prince some streets have only a faint light and many are not lit at all.

Nevertheless, the night is alive with people who are visiting, singing, strolling along the streets, or simply gathered together to gossip in squares or near house fronts. In the hilly country above Port-au-Prince, drums begin beating with a message: Tonight there will be a Voodoo ritual.

And yet, the ceremony that is about to take

place has been known about for a long time. Preparations for it have been going on for several months. The ceremony, for which the Petit family will pay and for whose benefit it is being conducted, has a very definite purpose.

About two years ago the Petits—grandfather, father, and sons—began to have difficulty with the crops on their land. Although they worked the land with great care and tried to improve their harvest, the amount of food produced was still considerably less than that being harvested by their neighbors. And then, almost without warning, two members of the family became ill and died within six months of each other.

It is at such a time as this that Haitians who are followers of Voodoo start to wonder if various forces have been set in motion to cause them harm.

Three possibilities are considered. One is that the family's loa feel they have not been shown the proper respect; they have not been given enough attention or have not been honored in the traditional ways. There is also the possibility that someone, probably an enemy of the family, has employed black magic in an effort to harm them. And finally, the family deceased may be displeased with their burials or the way their memory has been honored. Any one of these reasons is sufficient cause to begin the unlucky chain of events that has plagued the Petit family in recent years. As firm believers in Voodoo, they

In the dusk a group of drums hang ready for use. The drums are sacred and homage is paid to them during every Voodoo ceremony.

are certain that the only way to turn this evil tide is to hold a special Voodoo ceremony.

When the family reached a decision about their plan of action, the eldest member went to a local hungan to discuss the matter with him. Using his secret means to discover the cause of the problems in question, the priest decided on the kind of ritual that must be carried out. After he informed the Petit family of his plan, preparations were begun in the temple, or sanctuary, on the family compound rather than in the priest's own temple, which was several miles away.

Preparations for the Voodoo service began in the morning, although the effort to pay for the service began months previously. Many Voodoo services are very expensive and a family must save for months or even years in advance before the service can take place.

However, the Petit family considered this ceremony to be extremely important. They were glad to arrange and pay for the ritual that is now just a few hours away. Through the morning, tables to hold the offerings have been arranged, and now each is laden with eggs, cereals, cornmeal, and drinks—the foods that are relished by the loa. Nearby are chickens, roosters, and a goat, the sacrificial animals which will be slaughtered later in the evening.

Sometime during the afternoon the hungan arrived to make certain that everything was in order and that nothing was missing. He saw to it that the altar had its essential crucifix, pictures of Catholic saints, bottles of drinks, special gourds of flour, and other articles of this kind. Then he began to design the magical and decorative veves.

Now it is time for the ceremony to start. During

A Voodoo altar with the sacred asson in the foreground.

the first part of the ceremony Catholic prayers are said, a preliminary which is believed to "set the loa in motion." But gradually the Catholic elements of the ceremony give way to the Voodoo elements. The songs change. The drums take a different beat and the excitement mounts as the more dramatic parts of a Voodoo ritual begin. Now some of the food is put in dishes for the animals. An important event is about to occur.

Voodoo places great importance on the use of blood in its various rituals. Priests and priestesses, as well as those celebrating some rituals, will taste blood. Pigs, goats, chickens, and roosters are among the most commonly sacrificed animals, but on rare occasions bulls will also be sacrificed. It is believed that the loa will eat some of what is slaughtered and that some of them also like blood. For all of these reasons the sacrifice of the animals and the collection of blood is one of the important aspects of the Voodoo ritual.

The goats, chickens, and roosters are washed in water that has been made fragrant by leaves and flowers. The goat is dried with a clean white towel and perfumed. Next it is dressed in a bright-colored piece of velvet; another piece is tied to the base of its horns.

All of the animals are offered food and drink and they can only be sacrificed if they eat at least a portion of what is offered. Should an animal refuse to eat, it has "refused" to be killed and another animal is substituted. It is believed that the food which the animal eats increases its sacred powers and that when it is killed these powers will pass to the sacrificers.

The animals smell the food that is offered to

A Voodoo ceremony with typical ritual flags. In this ceremony white pigeons are among the sacrificial animals. Before the ritual is over, the pigeons' necks will have been wrung and some of their blood drunk by the participants.

them. Slowly the chickens begin to eat but for a few minutes it looks as though the goat will refuse its food. Then its pink tongue comes out and it begins to eat. Now the animals are considered the property of the loa and are ready for the sacrifice.

First, however, they are picked up by the priest and his assistants, who whirl them around and dance with them for a few minutes. The priest sings a long chant inviting the loa to come.

Now the people who are present take up the song and begin to dance. The drums, an essential part of every Voodoo ritual, fan the excitement that is mounting throughout the temple.

The drums used for the Voodoo dance have come to symbolize Voodoo itself. "Beating the drum" is an expression often used in Haiti to mean "celebrating the cult of the loa."

The skill of the drummers during a ritual is of the greatest importance. Drummers who are talented and sensitive can electrify the atmosphere at a Voodoo ceremony. It is said they produce or stop possession by skillful use of the drums. The drummers, who are always men, must have learned a great many rhythms and songs and they need to have enormous stamina.

Tonight the drummers seem to fall into a frenzy as they beat without interruption on their drums. At times their eyeballs turn back under their lids and a strange rattling gasp sounds in their throats. Their

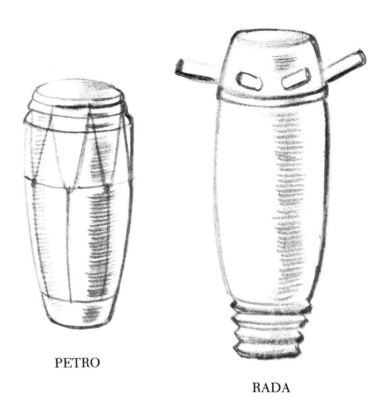

PETRO

RADA

Examples of Petro and Rada drums. The two types of drum are designed and decorated differently. Petro drums are always smaller than Rada drums. The latter are used in groups of three, the largest being called the Maman.

bodies seem to move without any directions from their brains.

Traditionally the Rada drums are never played

by themselves but in groups of three. They are different in size but not in design. The biggest drum, called the Maman, is more than a yard long. Each of the drums is beaten in a different manner.

The drums are sacred objects and the priest kisses the ground in front of them from time to time. Occasionally small offerings of clairin, home-brewed rum, are poured in front of them because it is believed that, like the loa, the drums need to be nourished if they are to keep their power and energy. They are also given food; even chickens are sacrificed to them.

But now some of the dancers are falling into odd positions. Their limbs move spasmodically and a strange look has come into their faces. The pupils of one woman's eyes have moved under her lids so that only the whites are showing. A few specks of foam have appeared at the corners of her mouth. She jerks and twitches uncontrollably and suddenly falls to the ground.

Meanwhile, as the other dancers continue to sing and dance, the hungan, with the help of his assistant, picks the woman up and carries her to a small room where clothes of the loa are kept. Since it is clear that this woman is being possessed by Baron Samedi, the Lord of Death, she is dressed in the clothes that are traditionally associated with him.

Long black trousers are pulled onto the woman's legs. A man's suit jacket is put on her torso while a battered black hat is stuck on her head. She is brought once again to the circle of dancers, where she is now greeted as the feared and respected Baron Samedi himself.

Toward midnight the animals are sacrificed, first the fowl and then the goat. On each animal the priest makes the mark of the cross with the knife and then the throat is slit. The blood is collected in a calabash and placed on the altar while the carcasses of the animals are piled in front of it.

The hungan makes a circle of cornmeal around the dead animals and then two white lines in a cross shape over them. He sings as he works and continues to sing until the ritual is finally finished and some of the women come to take the chickens for cleaning and cooking.

The goat is dressed by some of the men and cut into pieces. The head, feet, intestines, heart, liver, and kidneys of each animal are put into jars as food for the loa. They are buried in the ground while the remainder of the food is cooked for the Voodoo celebrants to eat.

While the food is being prepared, the music and songs continue. There is more dancing and once again some of the dancers go into trance. The familiar signs of jerking, twisting, and convulsion have overtaken some of the dancers. The loa are taking full possession.

Those who are possessed are completely in the

grip of the loa and are dancing with abandon. The priest dances opposite the possessed, never taking his eyes from them. There is a feeling of high tension and excitement in the temple now and the priest shows his recognition of the loa's presence by holding up a lighted candle in one hand and a container of water in the other. After a time he gives each of these to one of the possessed.

The dancers who hold the candle and water make their way to the central pole of the temple. There, the water is poured out and the sign of the cross is made with the candle. The same motions are repeated before the priest and the drums; the two dancers continue to dance in front of the drums while the other dancers move away to make more room for them.

The men who hold the rattles do not stay with the drummers but move with the crowd. They hold them high above the heads of the dancers and the sharp, steady sounds of the rattles are produced by faster and faster deft movements of the hands.

Usually the dancers who use the rattles are also strong singers who lead the group into new songs

As in many other religions throughout the world, water plays an important part in the Voodoo ritual. Often it is taken into the mouth of a mambo or hungan and sprayed in the four directions of the compass.

whenever the need to make a change occurs. Some of the songs can last for as long as twenty minutes.

Now it is almost dawn and the Voodoo dance and service are almost over. The loa have been appeased. They have eaten and drunk well. They have been shown in great detail how much the Petit family revere them. Because of this they will—according to believers in Voodoo—no longer bring harm to the Petits but will try to aid them in their various daily activities.

There is a feeling of contentment and satisfaction in the air as some of the dancers stop dancing and begin the journey home. The exhausted drummers stagger outdoors while young men take over the drums. In this way a good opportunity is given to hopeful musicians to try out their skills and prepare for the day when they will be professionals who play throughout the night at Voodoo rituals.

The apprentices play until dawn, when the last dancers wearily move into the cool morning air. Some of the dancers have been sleeping for several hours in different corners of the temple. Now they, too, rise from the floor and make their weary way home.

The Voodoo ritual just described is a general picture of what occurs during such a ceremony. The reader should know that ceremonies are greatly different from one another. Some rituals are basically social dances with only a few prayers offered and only a small dish of food and drink. At other rituals only one chicken may be sacrificed. Still others may be attended by large numbers of people, last several days, and involve the sacrifice of many animals.

All Voodoo ceremonies are developed from and refer to three basic plans or patterns of worship. The believer's age determines which plan shall be used for him or her, if a special ritual is necessary. The patterns are:

1. *Olo-kou-in-we.* From the ages of 1 to 10 the children of all believers in Voodoo are involved in this ritual which places the child under the protection of one aspect of the loa Legba.

2. *Olo-sih-se.* This plan applies to voodooists from the ages of 10 to 21. They are now under the care and protection of a different aspect of Legba. This is the time of the "mounting of the ritual water," which may be a symbol of developing adult sexuality.

3. *Olo-run-ti-te.* This plan concerns believers from the age of 21 until death.

Veve for Petro

5

THE HORRIBLE RED SECT

Few people in Haiti will talk about it. Not much is written about it. The average Haitian fears it as one of the most hideous and sinister encounters one can have in life. Several writers believe that it has no relation to Voodoo or is a terrible corruption of it. There are those who claim that it is a myth and has never existed. And yet the Sect Rouge, or Red Sect, has a long tradition in Haiti and some people insist that it operates today. Is the Sect Rouge related to the Voodoo Petro rite? A definite answer is impossible to find, although some people see a connection.

Rouge means "red" in French, a word which was applied to this group because blood, especially human blood, is of the greatest importance in their

rituals. Members of the Sect Rouge are also called
cochons gris—gray pigs or hairless pigs.

The sect originated in West Africa, where similar rituals and ceremonies have been practiced for
centuries. Like other aspects of Voodoo it was
brought to the Western Hemisphere by the slaves.

Membership in the Sect Rouge is highly secret.
It is thought that highly respected people in the community were once a part of it although their friends
and relatives have never found out they took part in
hideous rituals together with their fellow "gray
pigs."

What happens during a ceremony of the Sect
Rouge? Few people have witnessed such a horrible
ritual, but the various descriptions available to us are
quite similar. A meeting of the Sect Rouge always
begins during the late night hours, usually at a place
deep in the country and preferably in a secluded
place in the mountains.

Sometime during the earlier part of the evening
the high-pitched, insistent beats of a special drum
will have informed followers of the Sect Rouge
throughout the countryside that a meeting is to be
held. It is said that most people who hear the drum
will not know its special meaning because they have
not been initiated into the Sect Rouge.

However, those who are aware of the drum's
significance gradually assemble at the dark meeting
place. They will come dressed in their red—or occa-

sionally white—robes, or they will bring them in straw bags. Once they are together, they put on the garments and also add headwear in the shape of tin horns or straw hats with sharp tall crowns similar to those worn by witches in old prints. They may hold candles and whips which they crack in the air as they move in a column to a crossroads, a favored place for taking victims.

Here they make the all-important offerings of food, drink, and money to Maitre Carrefour (another name for Legba, Lord of the Crossroads). They beg him to help them in achieving success for the grisly activities they plan and then they move on to a cemetery. Here there are offerings to Baron Cimetiere, sometimes called Baron Samedi, who is Lord of the Cemetery. Once again prayers are spoken imploring assistance in the night's objective. The main goal of their prayers is to obtain a "goat without horns"—a human being—who can be sacrificed.

The hungan or mambo dances around the graves and makes crosses on them with clairin. They put candles and bowls of blood on top of the graves. Once the prayers and rituals have been properly observed, the "column" of the Sect Rouge combs the countryside for a victim. It is fear of the Sect Rouge that keeps people off the streets in Haiti late at night. No Haitian will venture out then unless it is absolutely necessary.

When the column of the Sect Rouge leaves the

cemetery it heads once again for a crossroads, a bridge, or some other place where there is a chance of meeting a passerby. Some of the members explore the area separately; each is supposed to carry a cord made from dried, cured human intestines which have come from victims who died in previous raids.

Now a peasant comes hurrying along the road on his way home. He was forced to work overtime at the port where he is employed as a laborer and he thinks of the trip home with fear as he hurries along looking neither to the left or right. But when he comes to the bridge he is easy prey and, as members of the Sect Rouge suddenly grasp him, he calls out desperately. Quickly, rags are stuffed into his mouth while the cord of intestines is wound around his neck.

The trembling victim is taken to a secluded clearing where highly secret incantations are spoken over him. These words are supposed to turn him into an animal, after which he is quickly killed with the swift strokes of a large sharp knife.

Belief in the ability of the sect's members to turn their victims into beasts ready for slaughter is widespread in Haiti. Some of the animals that come to slaughterhouses are thought to be human beings who have been magically transformed into beasts. You can tell such victims, it is said, by the especially sad expression in their eyes.

The poor traveler who was caught on the bridge is now being carved into several pieces. His flesh and blood provide food and drink for the members of the Sect Rouge. They believe it is only through this ritual that they can maintain their special powers. The ritual also keeps them a united force, committed to the same goals.

The gray pigs' victims are not always killed at once. Sometimes they are asked if they want to "come in or go out." This means they have the choice of going out at once (being killed) or of coming in—joining the Sect Rouge.

If the poor victim chooses to come in, he must drink a glass of human blood. He must also agree to "give" someone who is very dear to him to the Sect Rouge. One of the well-known stories about the giving of a loved one concerns a woman who agreed to sacrifice her son, a child of about fifteen.

Before she could act, however, another woman, presumably a member of the Sect Rouge, told the boy that a woman would try to lure him into the country. She told him to bow very low and throw a bucket of water over the woman while saying, "Greetings, Queen." That evening the boy was approached by a woman who was disguised and was accompanied by some odd-looking people. As instructed, the boy greeted the woman and poured the water over her head. She fell dead at his feet and her companions fled into the darkness. When the boy lit a lantern and looked down at the woman he discovered he had killed his own mother.

With such techniques the Sect Rouge are supposed to trick some of those who say they wish to join.

What is the truth concerning the Sect Rouge? This is almost impossible to discover but most writers on Voodoo mention it and some discuss it in detail. There is much evidence to show that secret societies such as the Sect Rouge have existed in Haiti for centuries. However, because of the extreme secrecy regarding their activities it is difficult to know if they still go about their grisly work today.

There is no doubt that groups similar to the Sect Rouge have operated in many African countries; for centuries cannibalism was practiced widely and was known to be an important feature of life among the Mondongues. Since many slaves from this tribe were brought to the Western Hemisphere it is likely that they brought knowledge of the secret societies with them.

Many Voodoo experts claim that the Sect Rouge is dominated by criminals and psychopathic persons who try to hide their sinister desires under the mask of Voodoo. They say that the sect is little more than an excuse to participate in subhuman activities that destroy life in a merciless fashion.

Perhaps no one can know the truth about the Sect Rouge until they have some experience of it. But such a possibility can exist only for the most adventuresome—or foolhardy.

6

ZOMBIES AND THE REALM OF DEATH

Death is a very important event for believers in Voodoo. Since those who have died can affect the lives of the living for both good and evil, much attention is given to the rituals which take place at the moment of death. In Haiti the fear of the dead is so strong that even the poorest family will scrape up its last pennies to pay for a proper funeral when one of its members dies.

Believers in Voodoo place great importance on being close to other members of the family at the time of death. If a family member dies far from home great efforts will be made to bring the deceased person back.

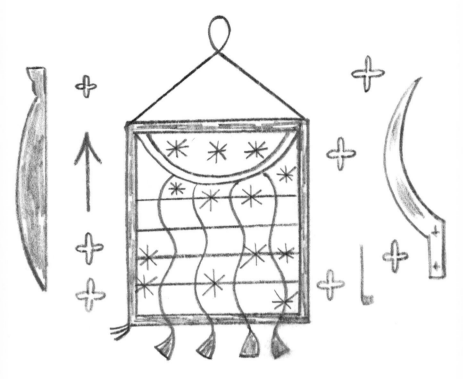

Veve for Azacca

Followers of Voodoo are convinced that everything possible must be done to please the dead. Should survivors forget or ignore their dead relatives, Voodoo teaches that the dead will take a terrible vengeance on the living.

In Haiti most people are part of what is called an extended family. Grandparents, parents, their children and grandchildren live in a group of houses on family-owned land in a family complex or compound.

Each compound has its own cemetery where members of the family are buried. It is common for big crosses to mark the graves. Although these might seem to be Catholic symbols recalling the cross of Christ, to believers in Voodoo they represent Baron Samedi, the loa of death. Family cemeteries are considered so important they are usually excluded from the sale of property. Many deeds state that cemetery plots will remain the sole property of the original seller no matter how many times the piece of land may be sold. In this way the spirits of the deceased from many generations can remain together and become a strong force when called upon for help.

Generally the dead do not disturb the living. But their goodwill can only be insured by three observances that must be practiced by the survivors. The survivors must first of all wear mourning clothes. They must arrange to have the loa taken from the dead person's head at death. And, finally, they must arrange for the dead to have a proper burial and grave. If they pay attention to the grave by keeping it neat and clean in the years following death, they win the favor of the deceased, who are glad to be remembered in this way.

Several other precautions must also be taken. True believers in Voodoo always rush to cover the clocks and mirrors in a room where a dead body is lying. They know that a spirit becomes very destructive when it sees either of these two objects. It is said that if this is not done the clocks will stop running for eternity and the mirrors will no longer have the power to reflect images.

Why is so much attention given to the dead? There are two reasons for this but they are not equally important. A proper and perhaps elaborate funeral insures that the family of the deceased will maintain or even gain in prestige in the community. Far more important is *fear* of the dead. Voodoo teaches that the dead who feel neglected and who believe they have not had a proper funeral can turn into vengeful, restless, discontented ghosts who will cause trouble for the survivors.

But this concern with death and the dead is not the same as the fear of zombies. The creation of a zombie is an infrequent aspect of death though it is one which is of concern to the average Haitian peasant.

Zombies are the living dead. They are the moving, breathing bodies of those without souls. They are bodies which have been resurrected from the grave by magical means. Zombies live only to do the will of others—a terrible fate which is greatly feared by the living.

Millions of people who know nothing of Voodoo are familiar with the idea of the zombie. The name itself is often applied to ordinary people who seem to have no will of their own, are thoughtless, and can be used by others. It would seem that most human beings are fascinated by the idea of complete domination of another and the destruction of his or her will; the zombie is the epitome of such a figure.

In Haiti and other countries where religions similar to Voodoo are strong, the fear of zombies is especially deep and pervasive. People fear that one day after their death they may become a zombie. They fear that a member of their family may become a zombie. Above all they fear the unexpected encounter with a zombie who may do them harm.

Anxiety about members of the family being turned into zombies is so strong that many families take great care to protect their dead after burial. Some families take turns sitting in the cemetery to keep watch for at least thirty-six hours after burial because it is believed that there is no possibility of revival after that.

Occasionally families have the bodies cut open and the hearts damaged so that absolute death is assured. Some people put a knife into the right hand of a corpse, believing that it will strike a blow to anyone who disturbs it on the first or second day of death.

Sudden or quick deaths, especially those of young people, are always suspect, and if a body stays warm after death it is a very bad sign. These are indications that the person has died from unnatural causes and that someone is hoping to turn the deceased into a zombie after burial.

Why would anyone want to cause another person to be a zombie? There are two main reasons why such a desire might exist. One is purely economic. It is believed that some people who have disagreeable, dirty work to be done do not want to hire laborers they must pay. Instead, they pay for the creation of zombies who are then in their control. Vengeance is another motive for seeking to make a dead person into a zombie. If the deceased caused pain, cheated, or committed other offenses, it is believed that the person who suffered at the deceased's hands will try to set the matter right after death by taking revenge.

According to an old legend about zombies, a typical experience might be the following: A rich farmer wants to buy some laborers for his farm as cheaply as possible. The farmer goes to the *bocor,* a magician, and makes an agreement with him. The bocor will know which people are sick and which are about to die. He performs the necessary ritual and when it is finished he mounts a horse, facing the horse's tail, and rides after dark to the house of the victim.

Quietly he slips up to the front door of the house, silently bends down and places his lips to the crack of the door. He sucks out the soul of the victim and rides off as fast as possible. Not long afterward the victim complains of feeling ill and soon he is dead. The bocor makes certain to watch the funeral in the cemetery from a safe distance. He never faces anyone in the mourning group but observes everything and then, at midnight, he returns to claim his victim.

Holding a special bottle in his hand, the bocor goes to the tomb of the deceased and calls the name of the victim. It is believed that, since the bocor holds the soul of the dead person, the deceased *must* answer when called.

Very slowly the dead person raises his head. As soon as the bocor sees this happening, he passes the bottle under the deceased's nose. Then he chains the victim's wrists and beats him on the head to awaken him more. Now the dead person rises and is quickly led from the tomb; the door to the tomb is locked behind him.

The zombie is taken to the Voodoo temple in a half-waking state. On the way he is taken past the house where he lived, a stage in gaining control of a zombie which is thought to be most important. If this is not done the victim might pass his former house one day and remember that he had lived there. But if he is taken there the memory of his home is supposed to leave his mind forever.

Once the corpse is in the Voodoo temple it is given a drop of liquid made from a highly secret formula. That is the final act which must be observed in the process of creating a zombie. From then on the zombie will work endlessly without being aware of his surroundings and he will not be conscious of himself. He will have no memory of who he once was, who his family was, or anything about his previous life or home. According to tradition, a zombie will not be able to speak again unless he is given salt.

Here is a famous story about a zombie that has been told in Haiti for years. It is believed to be true by many people.

At the end of the nineteenth century there lived a woman in northern Haiti who had a well-educated son. She adored and pampered him. She had spoiled him since he was an infant and refused to believe that he could do anything bad. However, as a young man he became involved in a love affair with a girl, which led to her pregnancy.

The young man's mother refused to believe that he was responsible. The girl's family became angry, claimed that only this man could possibly have fathered the child, and demanded that he marry her. But nothing could change the mother's attitude.

Two weeks later the young man became ill and died quickly. He was buried without any special precautions being taken. Several weeks later his mother was walking near the edge of town, lost in grief, when she saw some laborers loading ox carts with bags of coffee. She was astonished to see her son working in silence with these other men. All of them were being forced to work fast by a cruel foreman. The young man saw his mother but showed no sign that he recognized her. She became uncontrollable, rushed up to him, and screamed out his name. But as soon as she was about to embrace him, the foreman ran over and drove her away.

Frantically she ran for help but could not find any. She ran up and down streets, begging people to return with her. No one would accompany her and when she returned only the foreman was to be seen. He denied that any person fitting her son's description had been there. The mother never saw her son again although she continued to wander through the same area until she died a few years later.

In her book *Tell My Horse,* Zora Neale Hurston tells of a conversation with Dr. Rulx Leon, who was the director general of the Haitian Hygiene Service, about a zombie who had been found on the road and taken to the hospital.

Ms. Hurston became so interested in the story that she asked Dr. Leon's permission to investigate. He gave her a letter to the director of the hospital and requested that she be given full cooperation.

After the visit she wrote, "We found the zombie in the hospital yard. They had set her dinner before her but she was not eating. She hovered against the fence in a sort of defensive position. The moment she sensed our approach, she broke off a limb of a shrub and began to use it to dust and clean the ground and the table which bore her food. She showed . . . every sign of fear and expectation of abuse and violence . . . she seemed to hear nothing. Just kept trying to hide herself."

The poor woman kept hiding her head under a cloth and tried to move away from her visitors but they insisted on investigating and finally the doctor succeeded in taking the cloth off of her head. "The sight was dreadful," writes Ms. Hurston. "That blank face with the dead eyes. The eyelids were white all around the eyes as if they had been burned with acid. . . . There was nothing that you could say to her or get from her except by looking at her and the sight of this (human) wreckage was too much to endure for long. . . . We discussed at great length the theories of how zombies come to be. It was concluded that it was not a case of awakening the dead, but a matter of the semblance of death induced by some drug known to a few."

Ms. Hurston does not suggest that the woman described may have been in a severe psychopathological state, but from her description this seems a likely possibility. Perhaps *all* the stories about zombies are really descriptions of unfortunate people who are suffering from severe psychoses or other mental problems. In the past, mental illness was so poorly understood that the work of a devil, witch, or other supernatural force was thought to be the cause. And yet, as we have said before, the world is full of many mysteries that are still to be solved. Only scientific studies of the phenomenon of the zombie will show us if there is any truth to these old and terrifying legends.

Veve for Agasson

7
VOODOO
IN THE UNITED STATES AND MODERN HAITI

Voodoo never developed in the United States to the same extent as in the Caribbean, but it did gain a foothold in parts of Georgia, South Carolina, and Louisiana. One of the reasons for this was purely geographic. Most American plantations, unlike those in the West Indies, were on flat land. There were few opportunities for the slaves to practice Voodoo without the privacy that hill country like that of Haiti provided. American slaves also had much more contact with their white masters than those in the Caribbean. Their masters encouraged them to become interested in the Christian religion and to give up the beliefs they had brought from Africa.

The one stronghold of Voodoo in America was the city of New Orleans. The colonists saw how it flourished there and made many attempts to suppress it. In 1782, when Louisiana was still a Spanish colony, Governor Galvez banned the importation of slaves from Martinique because the people of that island were thought to be especially skilled in Voodoo.

Later many restrictions were placed on where blacks could meet. In the late 1830s blacks were forbidden to dance in Congo Square, which had long been a famous meeting place for the slaves of New Orleans. But somehow, ways were found to practice Voodoo. One of the most famous meeting places was the shore of Lake Ponchartrain, where thousands of Voodoo rituals were held throughout the nineteenth century.

In New Orleans itself, the practice of Voodoo took on a different character than in Haiti and other islands of the Caribbean. Although the religious rituals were still practiced, magic became the foremost concern. Some hungans and mambos, especially the latter, made fortunes because of the high prices they charged for their services. They sold charms and talismans and were especially concerned with the problems of love and vengeance.

It is said that some men paid large sums of money for a shell wrapped in a twist of human hair or a package of certain talcum powders, which they

A Voodoo doll, also called a talisman. The man and the cross signify that the Ghede loa— spirits of death—are masters of the events which will take place.

believed would help them win the love of a particular woman. Women, too, sought charms which would help them to gain the love of a man or to cause problems for a man's wife or lover.

During the nineteenth century many whites also became interested in Voodoo and some white women became mambos. But the importance of the loa and possession, of intercourse with the unseen worlds, became less important and the emphasis on magic continued to grow.

The Voodoo mambos who were believed to have

great power became widely known. Although there were many famous mambos in New Orleans, the best remembered is Marie Laveau. There is little factual information about her but her name appears in many books and newspapers of the period. We know for certain that she lived in the middle and latter part of the nineteenth century; although the newspapers reported her death in 1881, other reports claim that she lived until after World War I.

One of the reasons it is so difficult to find accurate details about her—or about other Voodoo "queens," as they were often called—is that Marie Laveau did not write about her powers or her life, and maintained strict secrecy about her experiences with her followers. All of her knowledge was passed on to her daughter, who took her name when she died.

Marie Laveau was a tall woman with thick curling black hair, of black, Indian, and white ancestry. Her father was said to have been a wealthy white plantation owner and her mother a mulatto with some Indian blood. Both Marie and her first husband, Jacques Paris, were free blacks. They lived at a time when New Orleans still had a strong French and Spanish character although it had been a part of the United States for sixteen years. The languages most frequently heard were French and Creole. During this period the colorful Quadroon Balls were at the height of their popularity and Indian squaws sold herbs, baskets, and other Indian wares in the market-place of the bustling and fast-growing city.

Marie and Jacques had been married only a short time when Jacques disappeared. Marie called herself the "Widow Paris" and went to work as a hairdresser. As beauty shops had not been thought of at this time, Marie went to the homes of wealthy women to do her work. She began to study the arts of Voodoo and she let it be known among her clients that she had special powers. By 1830 she was known throughout the city as the "Queen of New Orleans Voodoo."

Marie Laveau appears to have had a strong business sense. She was shrewd, determined, and well-organized. Sensing how strong belief in Roman Catholicism was in the people who came to her, Marie added many Catholic elements to her Voodoo rituals. She insisted that it was possible to be a good Catholic and a Voodooist at the same time. In this way she prevented many conflicts that might have arisen in those with strong Christian beliefs who were also attracted to Voodoo.

It is said that many charges were brought against Marie, but few ever reached the courts. Police attended her Voodoo rites and she was known to be the friend of city officials and other politicians. Whenever a serious problem arose she spoke to her influential friends about it and before long the problem no longer existed.

One of her most famous accomplishments involved a wealthy and prominent New Orleans family. The youngest son of the family had been arrested for a crime on the basis of strong evidence. His chances for release appeared so slight that the family appealed to Marie for help. They told her that she would have a very lavish reward if she could free their son.

According to the stories about this case, Marie went to the St. Louis cathedral at dawn and knelt at the altar rail for several hours with three Guinea peppers in her mouth. She then found her way into the judge's office and put the peppers under his chair. No one knows what prayers or incantations she used but her efforts were successful. The young man was freed, and Marie was given, as her reward, a small house on St. Anne Street, where she continued to live and practice Voodoo until her death.

The house on St. Anne Street was filled with people who came during the afternoon and late into the night. Marie grew famous for her skill in mind reading. As she grew older her knowledge of family secrets in New Orleans became even broader and her power, because of this knowledge, greater. Fantastic stories circulated throughout New Orleans about Marie's amazing abilities as a mambo.

Marie's apartments were often thronged with visitors from every class and section of New Orleans. Each was searching for love, money, health, revenge, or another personal objective. Politicians and political candidates would buy good luck charms—little objects made of wood, or bone supposedly dug from a graveyard—that would insure good fortune. Wealthy ladies paid high prices for amulets which would help them hold on to lovers.

It was the principle of "like to like" that determined what charm was to be used. Young girls who wanted to hold on to a lover were told to bring one of the man's gloves. Marie would then fill the glove with a mixture of steel dust, sugar, and honey. The steel dust was for power while the sugar and honey were supposed to sweeten the man. But the charm would work only if the girl slept with the glove under her mattress.

It was the Voodoo curse that was particularly feared by people who had some knowledge of Voodoo. They believed that it was stronger than the similar magic curses used throughout the United States and Europe. Being the object of such a curse inspired such terror and fear in the cursed that the emotions themselves could prove terribly destructive.

One of the most common curses was symbolized by a small black coffin with colored powders sprinkled around it. Often these were discovered by cursed persons on their doorsteps in the morning as they started off to work.

A small doll jabbed with pins or a wreath of black crepe fabric was also a sign that black magic was being employed to make someone die. Although

these grisly objects were sometimes left in plain view, it was often thought that they should be hidden on the property of the condemned person. This is why believers in Voodoo pay special attention to the hidden places in their houses—gardens, sheds, the areas under porches, or anywhere else where Voodoo objects of this kind might be left.

Voodoo has stayed alive in New Orleans and the area around it but on a much smaller scale than existed in the nineteenth century. Even today some people keep their front stoops very well washed because an old Voodoo tradition claims that washing the steps with a particular solution will destroy the effects of any evil objects which may have been placed on the steps.

Occasionally the newspapers report strange stories which undoubtedly have a strong Voodoo element. In 1953 a backcountry Southern farmer was arrested for the murder of two old women. He told police officers that they had put a hex on him by making a doll in his image and sticking pins into it. In 1960 a woman found a dead black cat with a cross on its back on her front steps.

A Haitian child holding a Voodoo doll. Although many hungans laugh at the idea of sticking pins into a doll, others say that techniques like this are used.

And special offerings are still put on Marie La-veau's tomb, especially on St. John's Eve, the most important Voodoo feast day.

The official attitude of the Haitian government toward Voodoo has varied through the centuries. Some of the earliest Haitian leaders, such as Tous-saint L'Ouverture, effectively used Voodoo to achieve their aims and then forbade its practice throughout the country. Perhaps they knew the power of Voodoo to dramatically change life and they feared its power might be used against them.

However, even when the official policy was strongly anti-Voodoo, ceremonies were allowed on national holidays and on religious festivals. Those in control of the government seemed to realize that the popular interest in Voodoo was so strong that it could not be completely destroyed. But the attitude of the Haitian upper classes was, and remains, negative to-ward the practice of what appears to them to be a primitive African cult.

A stepped-up drive against Voodoo was begun during World War I and, later, when American Ma-

A Voodoo ceremony for tourists. Rarely are Voodoo participants dressed in such costumes. And yet, ex-amples of genuine possession sometimes occur at rituals arranged for the benefit of tourists.

rines occupied Haiti, anti-Voodoo laws were strictly enforced. Anyone found conducting a Voodoo ceremony was sent to jail or given a heavy fine. Any mention of Voodoo in the press was censored and foreign journalists were discouraged from writing about it.

Then, in 1957, one of the strongest dictators Haiti had ever known came to power—Dr. François Duvalier, who was often referred to as "Papa Doc." In a strong effort to develop the country, he stressed black nationalism and sought any force or interest which would bring the citizens of Haiti together. President Duvalier had been interested in Voodoo for a long time and stirred up problems by trying to publish articles on it. When his word became law throughout the country, he encouraged Haitians to believe in the power of Voodoo and, in particular, to believe that some of his own power came from his knowledge of Voodoo.

When President Duvalier died, his place was taken by his son, Jean Claude Duvalier. He has continued his father's policies regarding Voodoo, which is practiced freely throughout the country today. In an interview with the author, President Duvalier said that he wished people throughout the world would eventually learn more about the true spirit of Voodoo and not merely its more sensational aspects. For this reason he encourages and supports scholarly studies of Voodoo and its effects on the people of Haiti.

Can Voodoo ceremonies be seen when visiting the island? That is a difficult question to answer. Some of the Voodoo rituals which the tourist is invited to see may or may not be authentic ceremonies. Frequently they are no more than convincing imitations cleverly enacted for groups of well-paying tourists.

However, one ceremony which is open to the public is conducted by the hungan Max Beauvoir; a highly regarded Voodoo priest, he has studied in France and the United States and has been awarded engineering degrees. Mr. Beauvoir, like President Duvalier, is interested in disseminating knowledge of Voodoo. When asked if a white person would ever be permitted to see a true Voodoo ceremony he replied that the color of one's skin has nothing to do with the question. According to Mr. Beauvoir, many black people are not permitted to witness certain Voodoo ceremonies because they have not been initiated into the mysteries of Voodoo. White people who wish to study Voodoo and participate in its ceremonies are free to do so. However, they must be prepared to undergo rites of initiation which are not always pleasant or easy to endure.

Voodoo offers its followers the fulfillment of what appear to be several basic human needs. The

desire to share in ritual, to participate in group ceremonies of a spiritual or religious nature, appears to be strong within many persons. Many human beings also feel the need to know more about, or try to make contact with, the unseen forces of the supernatural world. On still a different level, the human impulse to come together socially to share in the mutual enjoyment of song and dance, to find fulfillment through the esthetic experience of music and harmonious body movement, is basic to all people.

Modern society has forced men and women to find gratification of these needs in many different areas of life, but Voodoo offers the opportunity to satisfy them in one all-inclusive ceremony or ritual. Voodoo fulfills *all* of the needs described above. Whether it be called a cult, a folk religion, or a society of magicians, it is a potent, living force for millions of people who are sustained, supported, and uplifted by it.

Max Beauvoir, hungan of Port-au-Prince, standing in front of a decorative veve for Erzulie. Mr. Beauvoir, who holds degrees from universities in the United States and France, hopes to help change the misconceptions held by many people about Voodoo.

GLOSSARY OF VOODOO TERMS

AS·SON
A ritual gourd rattle made of a calabash and encased in strands of snake vertebrae. It is the property of hungans and mambos and is used in all important ceremonies.

BO·COR (Also BO·KOR)
A practitioner of magic.

CON·GO
One of the three Voodoo rites.

CRE·OLE
A person of French and native or Spanish and native descent born in the West Indies, Spanish America, or one of the early French or Spanish colonies, such as Louisiana. Also refers to a language which is a combination of French, African languages, and some Indian words.

DA·HO·MEY
One of the main geographical areas in Africa from which Haitian slaves were imported.

HOUN·GEN·I·CON (Also HOUN·GEN·I·KON)
A hungan's chief assistant.

HUN·GAN (Also HOUN·GAN)

A Voodoo priest. Derived from two Fon words: *houn,* meaning "spirit"; *gan,* meaning "chief."

KAN·ZO
Initiation into Voodoo.

LA PLACE
One of the assistants to a hungan.

LOA (pronounced LE·WA)
The deities or gods of Voodoo.

MAM·BO
A Voodoo priestess.

OUM'·PHOR
A Voodoo temple.

PER·I·STYLE
An enclosure with a roof but no walls where Voodoo dancing and some rites take place.

PET·RO
A group of Voodoo gods. Also the name of one of the three Voodoo rites.

RA·DA
The most commonly practiced Voodoo rite.

SECT ROUGE
A sect which is believed to practice human sacrifice, said by some authorities to be an offshoot of Voodoo.

VE·VE
Ritual maize flour drawing.

VOO·DOO
A folk religion practiced by people of the West Indies, primarily Haiti. Synonymous with Voudun, Vodun, Hoodoo.

ZOM·BIE
The walking dead. A dead body resurrected from the grave, deprived of its soul, and placed totally under the control of a living person.

SUGGESTIONS FOR FURTHER READING

Courlander, Harold. *Haiti Singing.* Chapel Hill: The University of North Carolina Press, 1939

Haskins, James. *Witchcraft, Mysticism and Magic in the Black World.* New York: Doubleday & Co., 1974

Herskovits, Melville J. *Life in a Haitian Valley.* New York: Doubleday & Co., 1971

Hurston, Zora Neale. *Tell My Horse.* Philadelphia: J. B. Lippincott Co., 1938

Metraux, Alfred. *Voodoo in Haiti.* New York: Schocken Books, 1972

INDEX

INDEX

ABOUT THE AUTHOR

KYLE KRISTOS' interest in Voodoo is a natural result of his lifelong studies in parapsychology. After several visits to Haiti, he became convinced that few places in the world offered so many opportunities to research paranormal behavior and psychic phenomena. He plans to return to Haiti to begin documented research on the mysterious powers possessed by initiates in Voodoo. Mr. Kristos lives in New York City.